A TRIP TO THE DENTIST

By Jodi Rawlinson

Library For All Ltd.

A Trip to the Dentist

First published 2023

Published by Library For All Ltd
Email: info@libraryforall.org
URL: libraryforall.org

Our Yarning logo design by Jason Lee, Bidjipidji Art

Original illustrations by keishart

A Trip to the Dentist
Rawlinson, Jodi
ISBN: 978-1-922991-96-6
SKU03385

A TRIP TO THE DENTIST

We respect and honour Aboriginal and Torres Strait Islander Elders past, present and future. We acknowledge the stories, traditions and living cultures of Aboriginal and Torres Strait Islander peoples on this land and commit to building a brighter future together.

Ruby bites down on her apple and feels a big pain in her tooth.

"OWW!" she cries out.

Ruby calls for her mum and shows her the sore tooth.

"MUM!"

Mum takes Ruby to
the dentist to check
her teeth.

The dentist tells Ruby
brushing your teeth every day
will keep the germs away.

BRUSH! BRUSH!

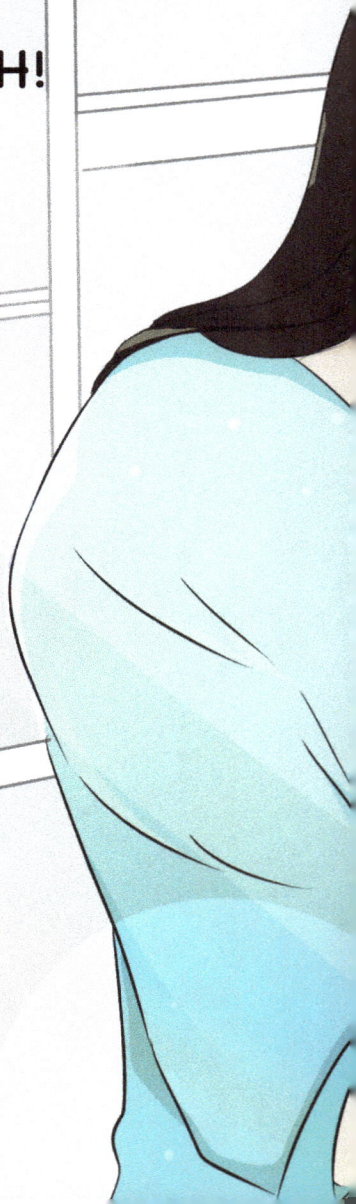

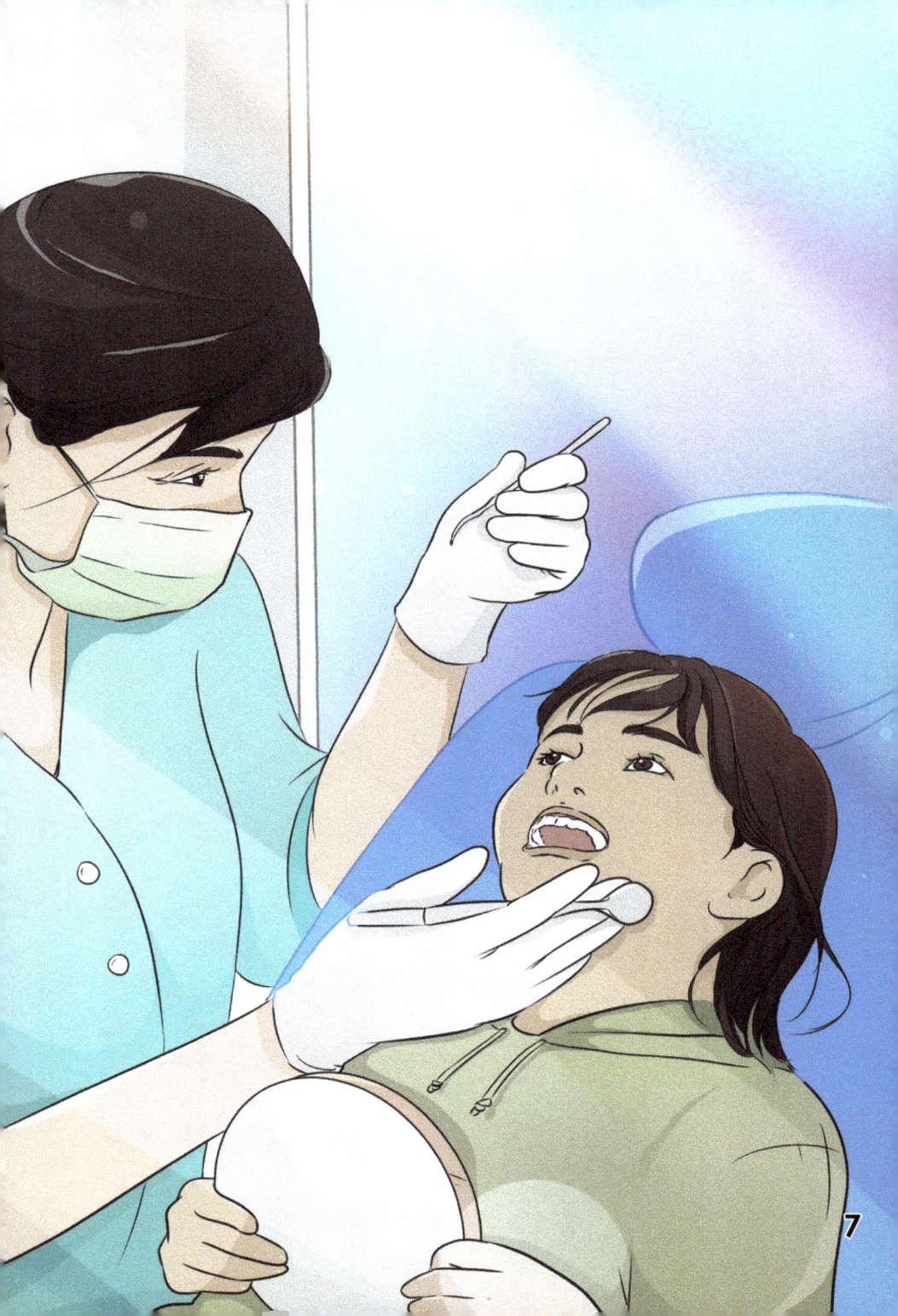

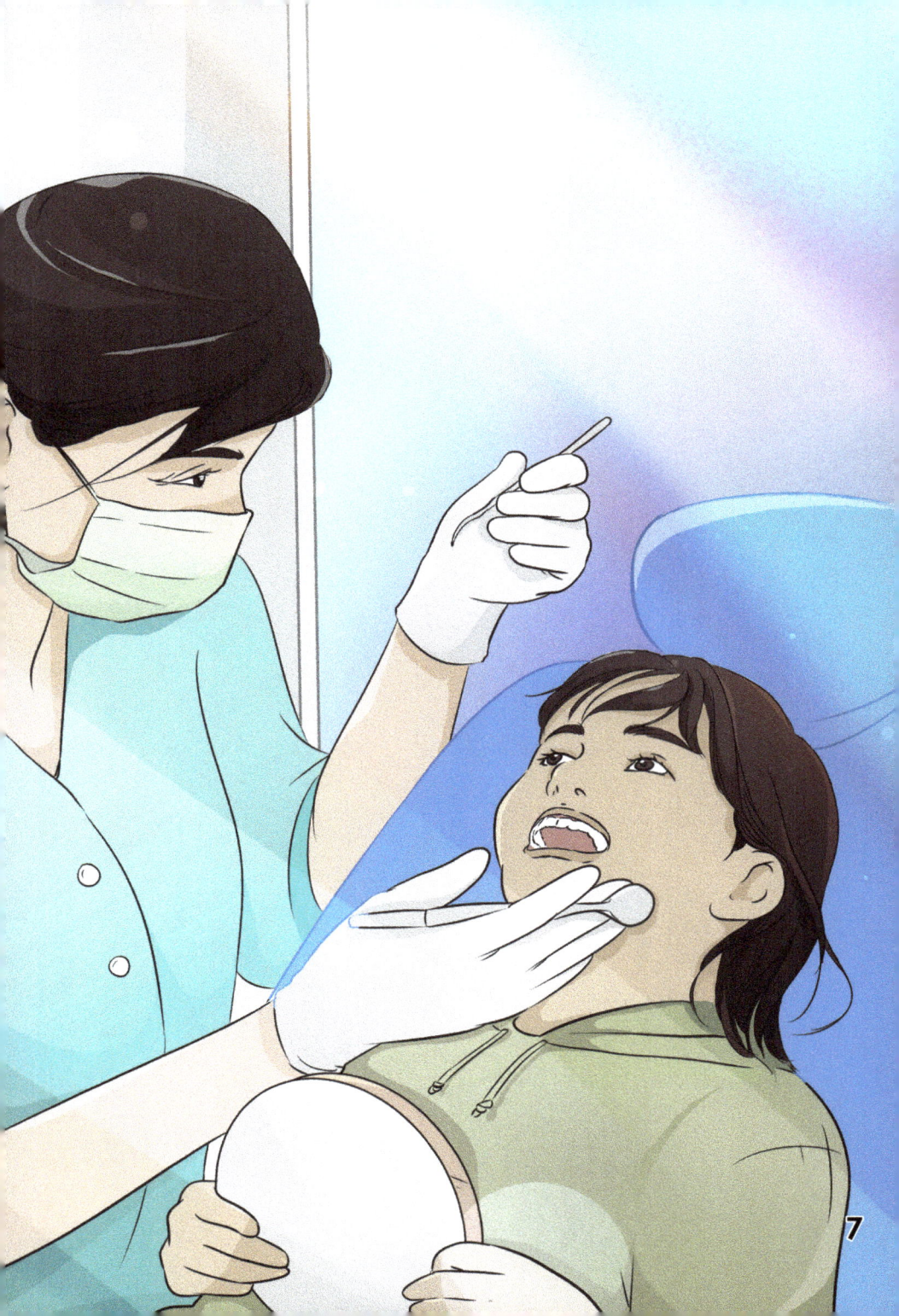

The dentist shows Ruby
how to hold the toothbrush
and make sure it reaches all
her teeth properly.

Ruby brushes her teeth,
just like the dentist
showed her.

SWISH, SWISH!
She rinses her mouth.

Ruby spits out the water and
smiles as the dentist says,
"Great job!"

When Ruby gets home, she shows her little sister how to brush her teeth properly.

Ruby and her sister are glad their teeth are clean and not hurting.

Do you brush your teeth properly and keep them clean?

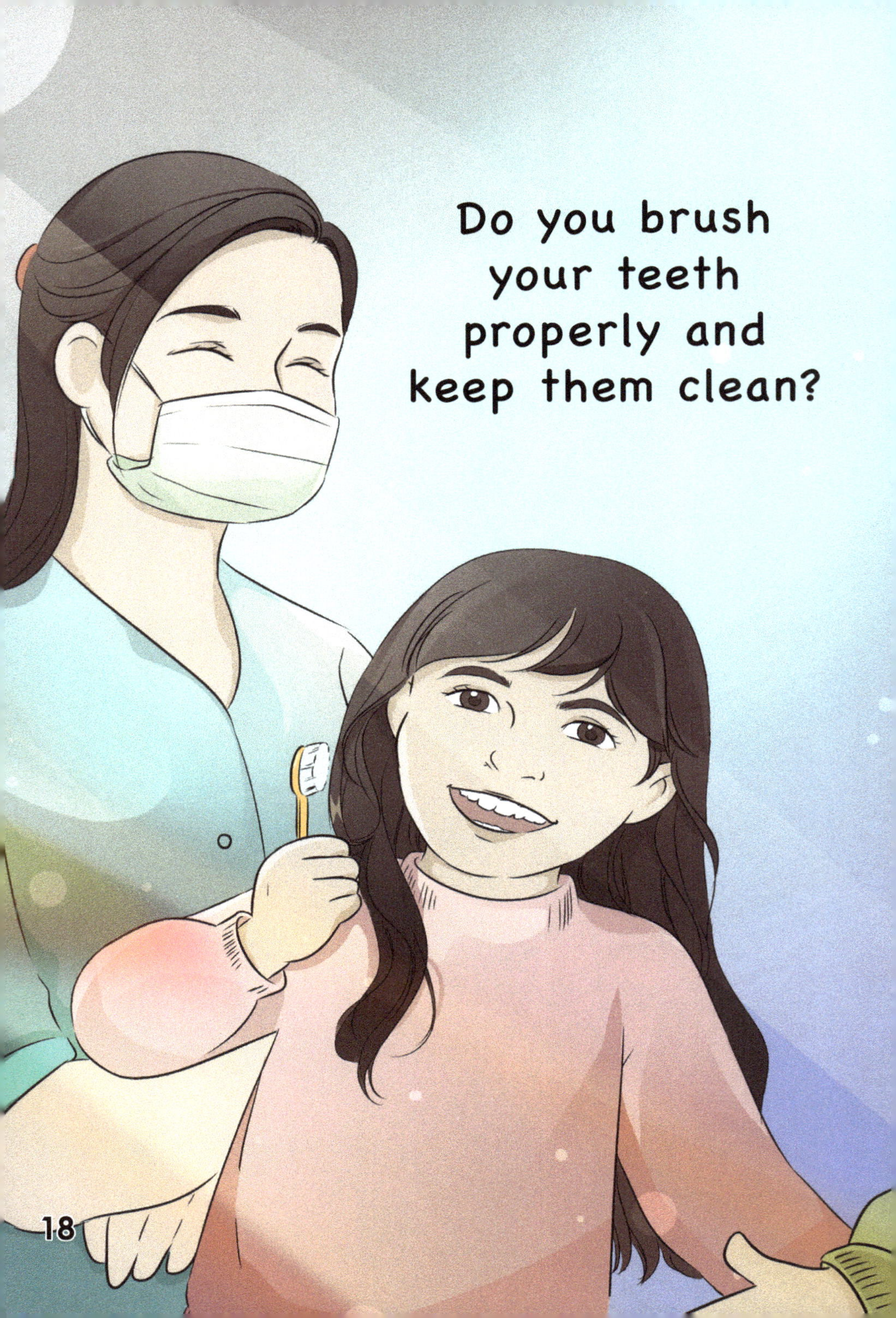

You can use these questions to talk about this book with your family, friends and teachers.

What did you learn from this book?

Describe this book in one word. Funny? Scary? Colourful? Interesting?

How did this book make you feel when you finished reading it?

What was your favourite part of this book?

About the author

Jodi was born in Adelaide and is from the Arrernte, Warlpirri and Torres Strait Islander Nations. She lives in Canberra and loves gardening and reading. When Jodi was younger, she loved reading *Alice in Wonderland*.

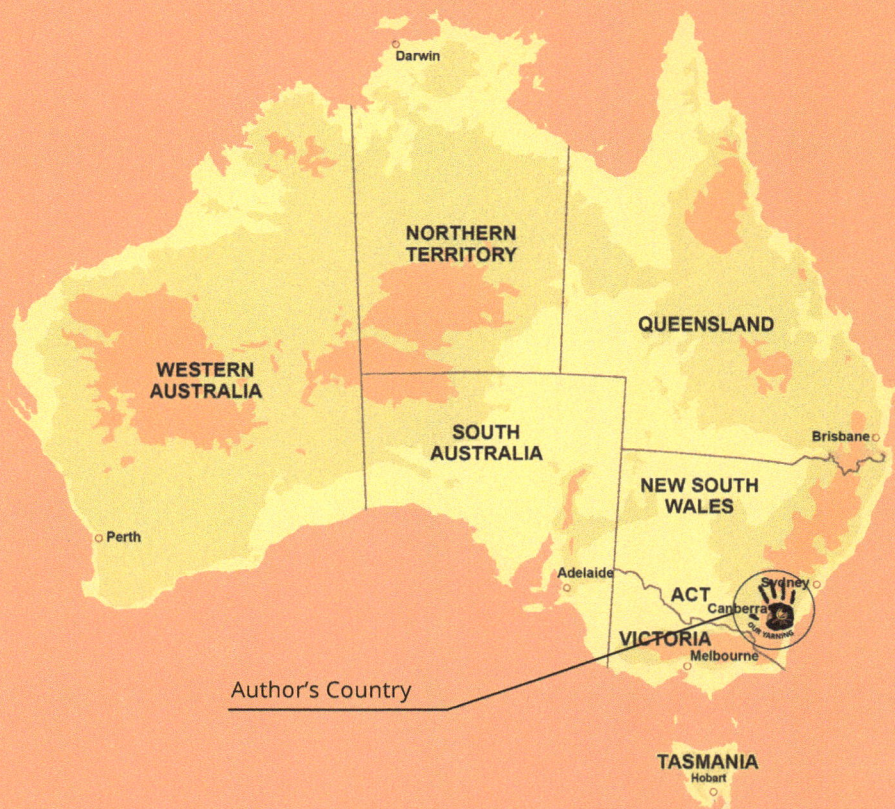

Author's Country

Our Yarning

Want to discover more books from this collection? Our Yarning is a collection of books written by Aboriginal and Torres Strait Islander peoples across Australia.

We know that children learn better, and enjoy reading more, when they see themselves in the stories, characters and illustrations of the books they read.

To download the app, visit the Google Play Store on any Android device and search 'Our Yarning'.

libraryforall.org

www.ingramcontent.com/pod-product-compliance
Lightning Source LLC
Chambersburg PA
CBHW042345040426
42448CB00019B/3418